Herkimer County
Community College Library
Herkimer, New York
13350

1. Books may be kept for three weeks and may be renewed once, except when otherwise noted.

2. Reference books, such as dictionaries and encyclopedias are to be used only in the Library.

3. A fine is charged for each day a book is not returned according to the above rule.

4. All injuries to books beyond reasonable wear and all losses shall be made good to the satisfaction of the Librarian.

5. Each borrower is held responsible for all books drawn on his card and for all fines accruing on the same.

THE DANISH AMERICANS

THE DANISH AMERICANS

Mark Mussari

CHELSEA HOUSE PUBLISHERS

New York   New Haven   Philadelphia

Cover Photo: Danish Americans in Omaha, Nebraska, celebrate the 75th anniversary of the state in 1929.

Editor-in-Chief: Nancy Toff
Executive Editor: Remmel T. Nunn
Managing Editor: Karyn Gullen Browne
Copy Chief: Juliann Barbato
Picture Editor: Adrian G. Allen
Art Director: Giannella Garrett
Manufacturing Manager: Gerald Levine

Staff for THE DANISH AMERICANS
Senior Editor: Sam Tanenhaus
Assistant Editor: Bert Yaeger
Copyeditor: Michael Goodman
Deputy Copy Chief: Ellen Scordato
Editorial Assistant: Theodore Keyes
Picture Researcher: PAR/NYC
Designer: Noreen M. Lamb
Layout: Louise Lippin
Production Coordinator: Joseph Romano
Cover Illustrator: Paul Biniasz
Banner Design: Hrana L. Janto

Creative Director: Harold Steinberg

First Printing

1   3   5   7   9   8   6   4   2

Library of Congress Cataloging-in-Publication Data

Mussari, Mark.
   The Danish Americans.

   (The Peoples of North America)
   Bibliography: p.
   Includes index.
   Summary: Discusses the history, culture, and religion of the Danes, factors encouraging their emigration, and their acceptance as an ethnic group in North America.
   1. Danish Americans.   2. Denmark—Emigration and immigration.   [1. Danish Americans]   I. Title.
II. Series.
E184.S19M87   1987   973'.043981   87-6541
ISBN 0-87754-871-4

CONTENTS

THE PEOPLES OF NORTH AMERICA

CHELSEA HOUSE PUBLISHERS

A
NATION
OF
NATIONS

Daniel Patrick Moynihan

The Constitution of the United States begins: "We the People of the United States . . ." Yet, as we know, the United States is not made up of a single group of people. It is made up of many peoples. Immigrants from Europe, Asia, Africa, and Central and South America settled in North America seeking a new life filled with opportunities unavailable in their homeland. Coming from many nations, they forged one nation and made it their own. More than 100 years ago, Walt Whitman expressed this perception of America as a melting pot: "Here is not merely a nation, but a teeming Nation of nations."

Although the ingenuity and acts of courage of these immigrants, our ancestors, shaped the North American way of life, we sometimes take their contributions for granted. This fine series, *The Peoples of North America,* examines the experiences and contributions of the immigrants and how these contributions determined the future of the United States and Canada.

Immigrants did not abandon their ethnic traditions when they reached the shores of North America. Each ethnic group had its own customs and traditions, and each brought different experiences, accomplishments, skills, values, styles of dress, and tastes in food that lingered long after its arrival. Yet this profusion of differences created a singularity, or bond, among the immigrants.

The United States and Canada are unusual in this respect. Whereas religious and ethnic differences have sparked intolerance throughout the rest of the world—from the 17th-century religious wars to the 19th-century nationalist movements in Europe to the near extermination of the Jewish people under Nazi Germany— North Americans have struggled to learn how to respect each other's differences and live in harmony.

Millions of immigrants from scores of homelands brought diversity to our continent. In a mass migration, some 12 million immigrants passed through the waiting rooms of New York's Ellis Island; thousands more came to the West Coast. At first, these immigrants were welcomed because labor was needed to meet the demands of the Industrial Age. Soon, however, the new immigrants faced the prejudice of earlier immigrants who saw them as a burden on the economy. Legislation was passed to limit immigration. The Chinese Exclusion Act of 1882 was among the first laws closing the doors to the promise of America. The Japanese were also effectively excluded by this law. In 1924, Congress set immigration quotas on a country-by-country basis.

Such prejudices might have triggered war, as they did in Europe, but North Americans chose negotiation and compromise, instead. This determination to resolve differences peacefully has been the hallmark of the peoples of North America.

The remarkable ability of Americans to live together as one people was seriously threatened by the issue of slavery. It was a symptom of growing intolerance in the world. Thousands of settlers from the British Isles had arrived in the colonies as indentured servants, agreeing to work for a specified number of years on farms or as apprentices in return for passage to America and room and board. When the first Africans arrived in the then-British colonies during the 17th century, some colonists thought that they too should be treated as indentured servants. Eventually, the question of whether the Africans should be viewed as indentured, like the English, or as slaves who could be owned for life, was considered in a Maryland court. The court's calamitous decree held that blacks were slaves bound to lifelong servitude, and so were their children.

America went through a time of moral examination and civil war before it finally freed African slaves and their descendants. The principle that all people are created equal had faced its greatest challenge and survived.

Yet the court ruling that set blacks apart from other races fanned flames of discrimination that burned long after slavery was abolished—and that still flicker today. The concept of racism had existed for centuries in countries throughout the world. For instance, when the Manchus conquered China in the 13th century, they decreed that Chinese and Manchus could not intermarry. To impress their superiority on the conquered Chinese, the Manchus ordered all Chinese men to wear their hair in a long braid called a queue.

By the 19th century, some intellectuals took up the banner of racism, citing Charles Darwin. Darwin's scientific studies hypothesized that highly evolved animals were dominant over other animals. Some advocates of this theory applied it to humans, asserting that certain races were more highly evolved than others and thus were superior.

This philosophy served as the basis for a new form of discrimination, not only against nonwhite people but also against various ethnic groups. Asians faced harsh discrimination and were depicted by popular 19th-century newspaper cartoonists as depraved, degenerate, and deficient in intelligence. When the Irish flooded American cities to escape the famine in Ireland, the cartoonists caricatured the typical "Paddy" (a common term for Irish immigrants) as an apelike creature with jutting jaw and sloping forehead.

By the 20th century, racism and ethnic prejudice had given rise to virulent theories of a Northern European master race. When Adolf Hitler came to power in Germany in 1933, he popularized the notion of Aryan supremacy. "Aryan," a term referring to the Indo-European races, was applied to so-called superior physical characteristics such as blond hair, blue eyes, and delicate facial features. Anyone with darker and heavier features was considered inferior. Buttressed by these theories, the German Nazi state from

1933 to 1945 set out to destroy European Jews, along with Poles, Russians, and other groups considered inferior. It nearly succeeded. Millions of these people were exterminated.

The tragedies brought on by ethnic and racial intolerance throughout the world demonstrate the importance of North America's efforts to create a society free of prejudice and inequality.

A relatively recent example of the New World's desire to resolve ethnic friction nonviolently is the solution the Canadians found to a conflict between two ethnic groups. A long-standing dispute as to whether Canadian culture was properly English or French resurfaced in the mid-1960s, dividing the peoples of the French-speaking Quebec Province from those of the English-speaking provinces. Relations grew tense, then bitter, then violent. The Royal Commission on Bilingualism and Biculturalism was established to study the growing crisis and to propose measures to ease the tensions. As a result of the commission's recommendations, all official documents and statements from the national government's capital at Ottawa are now issued in both French and English, and bilingual education is encouraged.

The year 1980 marked a coming of age for the United States's ethnic heritage. For the first time, the U.S. Census asked people about their ethnic background. Americans chose from more than 100 groups, including French Basque, Spanish Basque, French Canadian, Afro-American, Peruvian, Armenian, Chinese, and Japanese. The ethnic group with the largest response was English (49.6 million). More than 100 million Americans claimed ancestors from the British Isles, which includes England, Ireland, Wales, and Scotland. There were almost as many Germans (49.2 million) as English. The Irish-American population (40.2 million) was third, but the next largest ethnic group, the Afro-Americans, was a distant fourth (21 million). There was a sizable group of French ancestry (13 million), as well as of Italian (12 million). Poles, Dutch, Swedes, Norwegians, and Russians followed. These groups, and other smaller ones, represent the wondrous profusion of ethnic influences in North America.

Canada, too, has learned more about the diversity of its population. Studies conducted during the French/English conflict showed that Canadians were descended from Ukrainians, Germans, Italians, Chinese, Japanese, native Indians, and Eskimos, among others. Canada found it had no ethnic majority, although nearly half of its immigrant population had come from the British Isles. Canada, like the United States, is a land of immigrants for whom mutual tolerance is a matter of reason as well as principle.

The people of North America are the descendants of one of the greatest migrations in history. And that migration is not over. Koreans, Vietnamese, Nicaraguans, Cubans, and many others are heading for the shores of North America in large numbers. This mix of cultures shapes every aspect of our lives. To understand ourselves, we must know something about our diverse ethnic ancestry. Nothing so defines the North American nations as the motto on the Great Seal of the United States: *E Pluribus Unum*—Out of Many, One. ⮽

Some of Nebraska's early settlers, such as the Nelson family, who posed for this photo in 1895, were Danish-American immigrants.

A DEFT ADJUSTMENT

More than almost any other ethnic group, Danish Americans have found the United States to be the great melting pot of the world. Within a generation of their great migration in the late 1800s, most newcomers from Denmark had become full-fledged Americans. The majority had learned English and married outside their own group, inhabiting communities throughout the United States and Canada.

Danish immigrants adjusted easily for a number of reasons. For one, they composed a small ethnic population, compared with their fellow newcomers from Scandinavia—Swedes and Norwegians. Second, many Danes had been well educated in their homeland and had little trouble learning English. Third, because the majority came to America for the purpose of owning land and earning a livelihood, instead of escaping political or religious persecution, Danes, as a group, felt little need to cling to ancestral traits or beliefs that might have slowed their progress in a new country. Finally, Danes, like the "Yankee" descendants of the original American colonists, were an Anglo-Saxon people. Thus, they quickly won the acceptance of their adopted homeland's most established and powerful ethnic group.

Gutzon Borglum, a Danish American, designed the Mount Rushmore National Memorial, completed in the 1940s.

Unlike many other immigrant groups, Danes showed little interest in forming their own communities. Only a few Danish settlements, small towns scattered mostly in the Midwest, featured ethnic churches, social organizations, and schools, though Danish-American "folk" high schools constituted Denmark's most important contribution to American culture. In short, no place in America can be considered a Danish community, per se. Even in the areas where the majority of Danish Americans clustered, they often were a minority population. In consequence, their *danskhed*—their "Danishness"—disappeared rather quickly as they blended into the American mainstream.

This lack of ethnic visibility worked both for and against Danish Americans. They managed to avoid the stereotypes applied to other nationalities, but at the same time their role in American life was overshadowed by those of other groups more interested in maintaining their unique identities. Many examples of prominent Italian, Jewish, Chinese, or African Americans come readily to mind, but most people find it difficult to name a single, recognizable Danish American. Few New Yorkers realize that the Bronx was actually named after an early Danish settler, Jonas Bronck. Two million people annually visit Mount Rushmore, one of America's most celebrated national monuments, yet hardly any are aware that it is the creation of Gutzon Borglum, a Danish American.

Danish Americans remain a fairly small ethnic group. According to the 1980 census, only 1,518,273 Americans reported some Danish ancestry (as compared to more than 20 million Irish Americans). An even smaller number—426,619—claimed to be entirely of Danish descent. Moreover, many Americans of Danish ancestry maintain very few ties with one another or with Denmark.

Recently, however, Danish Americans have partaken in the ethnic revival shared by other ethnic groups. Some Danish-American organizations promote a sense of history—for example, the Danish American Heritage Association, founded in 1977. As more Danish Americans reclaim their ethnic roots, they gain an appreciation for the significant role their ancestors played in building the United States, along with an understanding that the Danish-American experience forms an indispensable piece of the complex and inspirational story of America's immigrants. ✒

DENMARK: THE LAND AND ITS HISTORY

To this day, the popular conception of Denmark is of an unassuming, almost quaint little country with a tradition of fine craftsmanship (its furniture is world-renowned) and of artistic achievement. Denmark's Hans Christian Andersen (1805–1875), for example, achieved recognition for his fairy tales, which have been translated into most languages. At different times in its long history, however, Denmark was a major empire and stood at the apex of the largest unified kingdom in Europe.

The Link to the Continent

For centuries, Denmark's location enabled it to exercise influence far in excess of its size. The southernmost country of Scandinavia—an area of northern Europe that also includes Norway, Sweden, Finland, and Iceland—Denmark consists of the Jutland peninsula and of more than 400 adjacent islands. This chain of islands reaches almost to the Swedish coast. At the same time, Denmark is the only Scandinavian country with a land link to the European continent—the 42-mile border between Jutland and West Germany.

The three-sided Jellinge stone records milestones of the 10th-century rule of Harald Bluetooth.

Denmark also profits from being surrounded by the North and Baltic seas. As the "gatekeeper" of the latter body of water, Denmark sits at the entrance of the major northern shipping route between eastern and western Europe. It is thus strategically situated at the crossroads of trade—both north-south and west-east—a position that has played a fundamental role in its development as a civilization.

Though Denmark is only one-third the size of New York State, the indentations of its scalloped coastline add up to a total of 4,500 miles, and no part of the country is more than 30 miles from the sea. It is not surprising then that the sea has often determined Denmark's role in world affairs. The country's naval power has dictated its national strength during periods as diverse as the 9th-century Viking conquests and the mercantile and colonial triumphs of the 16th century.

Conversely, Denmark's darkest times often have been the consequence of naval defeats, such as England's bombardment of Copenhagen in 1807 and its subsequent capture of the Danish fleet.

Even when Denmark was not able to flex its muscles as a naval power, the nation continued to serve as an important passageway between Scandinavia and the Continent. Archeological evidence indicates that in prehistoric times, Denmark was the bridge for settlers migrating north from mainland Europe to Sweden and Norway. Later, in the 9th century, it was the Scandinavian gateway to the treasures of Europe, which had attracted the attention of the era's fiercest warriors.

The Vikings

The first inhabitants of Denmark were probably nomadic hunters who roamed the region until about 10,000 B.C. During the following centuries, they formed agricultural settlements and, by 2000 B.C., a Bronze Age culture. Little is known about those eras or about the succeeding centuries of Danish history. Indeed, Danes made no visible impact as a people until about A.D. 800. At that time, a seafaring Scandinavian people, the Vikings—or Norsemen—began to raid and conquer large areas of Europe. The 9th to the 11th centuries are known today as the Viking era. Rival theories have sought to explain why the Vikings launched their raids. Some historians argue that they simply desired to loot other societies. Others suggest that their homelands had become overpopulated. Still others think that the Scandinavian climate had become sharply inhospitable to farming.

There is little disagreement about why the Viking voyages were so successful: their superior shipbuilding. Viking vessels weathered not only the seas but also the ages, and many can be viewed today in museums. The typical Viking ship was pointed at both ends—bow and stern—and could be propelled by both oars and sails.

Swift and stable on the high seas, such a ship could also be maneuvered easily and quickly in rivers and bays. It was exactly such a boat that carried Leif Eriksson, a Norwegian, to the shores of North America in A.D. 1000, nearly 500 years before Christopher Columbus.

The Danish Vikings usually followed western trade routes, warring and conquering wherever they landed. In the 10th century, Denmark became a united country under King Gorm, who ruled from North Jutland. Gorm's son Harald Blaatand (Bluetooth) continued to unify the country by converting the Danes to Christianity and annexing Norway. In 1013, the Viking king Svend Tveskaeg (Sweyn I Forkbeard) conquered England, and Svend's son, Canute, presided over a kingdom that extended into Sweden.

After the death of Canute in 1035, the empire crumbled and Viking influence waned. This decline also can be traced to revitalized Mediterranean trade routes, which cut into traffic passing through the north and

Vikings probably defended themselves by erecting forts much like this contemporary model.

In the 14th century, Queen Margaret urged Norway and Sweden to ally with Denmark and form the Kalmar Union.

reduced the number of ships that the Vikings could prey upon. In addition, the shape of society within Denmark was undergoing a crucial change. Tribal clans had begun to consolidate into stable nations that advanced and grew from within, similar to the feudal kingdoms of the European continent.

The Middle Ages

In 1375 the only political arrangement ever to unite the three major Scandinavian nations was negotiated by the sagacious Queen Margaret I, who became Denmark's regent when her son, Olaf I, acceded to the throne at the age of 5. Olaf died young, however, and Margaret

The German monk Martin Luther (far left) who founded Protestantism, meets with reformers in about 1543.

was elected queen of Denmark and Norway, and then of Sweden. At her urging, all three nations combined to form the Kalmar Union, which preserved the separate laws of each of the countries.

The Union was dominated by Denmark, the richest of the three countries and also the most populous, and its seat was Copenhagen, the Danish capital. Margaret preserved the balance of the Union by steering clear of war, without yielding territory to the Germans, who were becoming more powerful in the lands to the south. The Kalmar Union continued to govern northern Europe, thus enabling Denmark to become a nation of great influence. But by 1523, Sweden, which had grown increasingly nationalistic, abandoned the Union, initiating its decline. Denmark and Norway kept their partnership alive until 1814 when the Union was finally dissolved.

Church and State

A crucial factor in Denmark's emergence as a European power was its adoption of Roman Catholicism in the late 9th century. The church's economic might was formidable. One-third of the church's wealth was controlled by Danish bishops, who used it to strengthen their role in the country's political affairs. They were able to do this because the Danish government made bishoprics accessible only to members of the nobility. As a result, bishops came from the ranks of the well-to-do and were able to extend their financial influence by manipulating church finances for whatever purposes they deemed proper. A religious post became, in effect, a political and even military one.

By the mid-16th century, when Christian III assumed the throne, the church was sorely in need of massive reform. In Germany, a scholarly monk, Martin Luther, had written a treatise that severely criticized the widespread corruption of Roman Catholicism. Luther urged a reorganization of Christianity that diminished the role of the Pope and the ecclesiastical hierarchy that supported him. He denounced the sale of indulgences, which were thought to save the souls of the dead, and argued that the individual worshiper's faith and obedience to God should be more important than rituals conducted within the chapel.

Luther's reformist doctrines sparked intense controversy throughout Europe. His bold objections to es-

King Christian IV developed Denmark's industries but also sapped the country's resources by dragging it into the Thirty Years' War.

Prosperous citizens of Copenhagen sport their finery in this 17th-century engraving.

tablished church practices gained many followers, and the movement culminated in the Protestant Reformation, which split the Christian world in two. In Denmark, King Christian III, who was personally acquainted with Luther, transferred his allegiance from the Roman Catholic church to Luther. Before he could impose Lutheranism on his country, however, he still had to do battle with the entrenched Catholic faction. In 1536, King Christian's forces were victorious. The Catholic bishops were imprisoned and released only after submitting to the king's plan for reorganizing the church. They were stripped of their holdings, which proved so great that the confiscated property easily paid for all the debts owed by the monarch to various creditors.

Foreign Exploits

By the 16th century, Denmark was a prosperous commercial nation, its main source of income derived from duties levied on ships passing through the sound connecting the Baltic and North seas. Many European countries at this time were seeking to consolidate national power and wealth through strict governmental regulation of the entire economy.

This policy, mercantilism, was pursued in the 17th century by King Christian IV, who developed industries intended to produce goods for foreign export. He backed the formation of companies specializing in foreign exploration and trade. In order to expand Denmark's economic horizons, the king hired explorer Jens Munk to search the New World for a trade passage to the Orient. Though he never found the passage, Munk became the first Dane to reach the North American continent.

Denmark's busy marketplaces suffered during the economic setbacks of the 19th century.

Although responsible for many innovations, Christian IV eroded his country's wealth and resources by entering the Thirty Years' War and attempting to conquer the north German coast. Thus began a long series of battles, pitting Denmark against its neighbors. Denmark lost a third of its land and population in the protracted war, which culminated in 1660, when the Peace of Copenhagen drew the Danish, Swedish, and Norwegian frontiers close to their present boundaries, with Sweden reigning as the most powerful Baltic nation.

The Age of Social Reform

In the year 1700, Denmark was an absolute monarchy. Most of its resources lay in the hands of the crown, and the rest was possessed by wealthy landowners. Although Danish peasants composed 80 percent of the population, they owned only 2 percent of the land and were cruelly exploited by greedy nobles, who, among other outrages, prohibited peasants between the ages of

Denmark tried to remain neutral during the Napoleonic Wars, but English fleets devastated Copenhagen.

4 and 40 from leaving the district of their birth. It is not surprising that Denmark's agricultural output stagnated under these harsh conditions.

Beginning in 1786, three years before revolution broke out in France, Denmark averted a similar crisis by instituting land reform. Compulsory residence requirements were abolished, and the land was divided and apportioned among independent farmers. Those who actually worked the soil were finally allowed to own it, ending centuries of feudalism. Later, the School Law of 1814 provided free education for children between the ages of 7 and 14.

On the international level, Denmark stumbled in the 19th century, losing 40 percent of its territory and suffering from the migration of more than 300,000 citizens, many of whom went to the United States. These setbacks were caused by the Napoleonic Wars waged between France and Great Britain. Denmark tried to remain neutral, but was inevitably drawn into the conflict. Copenhagen was devastated, much of the Danish navy was destroyed, and Norway fell to Sweden. Trade was seriously disrupted, and in 1813 the Danish national bank declared bankruptcy.

Mid-19th-century social reforms included cooperative dairy farms, such as this one, established on the isle of Møn.

In 1848, revolution spread through Europe. This engraving depicts a mass protest in Copenhagen, where citizens demanded a more liberal constitution.

Social reforms continued, however. In 1849, King Frederick VII declared the end of the absolute monarchy. A parliament was established and its members were chosen by an electorate formed of landowners. Freedom of the press, assembly, and religion were granted, and people were given the right to form political parties. Women were not allowed to vote, however, until a new constitution was approved in 1915.

In 1864 Denmark, under King Christian X, lost almost one quarter of its territory. As many as 50,000 Danes fled their country when Slesvig, the southern part of Jutland, fell to the armies of Prussia, the German state then led by Otto von Bismarck, who saw to it that German territories were expanded in two subsequent wars that brought about a united German empire. After this blow, Denmark surrendered all hope of again becoming an influential European power.

In the late 19th century, economic depression struck and many farmers fled to America, the very country whose large, cheap grain exports ruined Denmark's agriculture by destroying its overseas markets. Some Danish farmers rebounded by switching to dairy production. Groups of small farmers banded together into cooperatives that sold their goods at low prices.

In 1871, the Social Democratic party was instituted in Denmark with the intention of establishing a government on socialist principles. Party membership was drawn mostly from the ranks of industrial workers, civil servants, and shopowners. Based on theories formulated in the mid-19th century by the radical German philosopher, Karl Marx, social democracy was intended to participate with existing governments rather than overthrow them. Later, Social Democrats were instru-

Women shop at Copenhagen's fish market in about 1900.

mental in organizing trade unions. Many Danish socialists eventually went to America and continued to work for political change there.

The Modern Era

Because Denmark's military defeats had led to its declaration of neutrality, the outbreak of World War I in 1914 had little immediate impact. But the war lasted longer than expected—until 1918—dealing death to millions with unprecedented destructive power. It also damaged the economies of many nations, Denmark among them. At the same time, however, the government continued to enact social reforms, including old-age pensions as well as health and unemployment insurance. Together, these changes laid the basis for the present Danish welfare state.

When Germany, which had initiated World War I, started to rearm in 1935 under the Nazi dictator, Adolf Hitler, Denmark realized it could not resist an attack by its powerful southern neighbor. In 1939, Denmark became the only Scandinavian country to sign a nonaggression pact proposed by Hitler. When war was declared in September 1939, Denmark quickly declared its neutrality, but on April 9, 1940, the Nazis marched into and occupied Jutland.

At first, Denmark was treated as a protectorate and the occupation had little effect on daily life. But German pressure increased. The Nazis demanded the persecution of Danish Jews and wanted to institute the death penalty for sabotage. When the Danish government resisted, the German army took over, and King Christian X was interned. The Danish army was disbanded, Danes were murdered, and Jews were seized and deported to concentration camps although some

King Christian X (mounted) won the admiration of his citizens by pinning a Jewish star to his chest and defying the anti-Semitic Nazi regime.

were hidden by their countrymen and smuggled to safety in free Sweden.

Outraged Danes began a resistance movement. In September 1943, the Danish Freedom Council was formed and resistance activities multiplied to include illegal newspapers, spy networks, and sabotage. In 1944, a general strike protesting Nazi policies crippled Copenhagen. Even schoolchildren participated. A group of Jutland students began the Churchill Club, and became such successful saboteurs that they inspired an American comic strip series.

Perhaps the most remarkable act of resistance occurred after the Nazis, intent on singling out the country's Jews, ordered all of them to wear a yellow Star of David. King Christian X, the leader of the state Lu-

Contemporary Danes stroll along The Stroeg, *Copenhagen's mile-long pedestrian boulevard.*

In 1964, old Denmark meets new during the inauguration of the Billun Airport, on the Jutland peninsula.

theran church, responded by riding through the streets displaying the star on his chest. By the end of the day, the citizens of Copenhagen, Jewish or not, wore the star, a courageous act of sympathy for the Jews and contempt for Nazi policies.

Denmark Today

Today, Denmark is a constitutional monarchy, in which the Danish king cooperates with Parliament to enact the nation's laws. The current queen, Margrethe II, came to the throne in 1972, thus maintaining Denmark's standing as the oldest monarchy in Europe.

Denmark is a prosperous country, with one of the highest living standards in the world. Its current population numbers about 5 million, 1 million of whom live in the capital, Copenhagen. The country's population has stabilized, as increases in life expectancy compensate for a declining birthrate. Denmark remains a remarkably homogenous country, and one of the most peaceful societies in the world. ❧

An engraving depicts Vitus Bering's expedition struggling in the icy seas off the Alaskan coast.

ARRIVING IN THE NEW WORLD

The largest Danish emigration to North America came in the late 19th century, but Danes have been present in the New World since the first days of colonization. Their numbers were quite small, however, and wherever they settled they were a minority. Many married outside the ethnic group, speeding up the process of adjustment to the New World and establishing a pattern of assimilation continued by later generations of Danish immigrants.

Two Early Explorers

Because the 16th century was a period of great industrial development in Denmark, King Christian IV was eager to find new trade outlets for Danish goods. At the time, Europeans were convinced that North America contained a sea passage to the Far East that would facilitate trade. With this in mind, the king commissioned Jens Munk (1579–1628) to find the hoped-for Northwest Passage. Though he never found the passage that would have led him through the arctic waters north of Canada, Munk and the 65 sailors who accompanied him became the first Danes to reach the New World. They entered Canada's Hudson Bay, proceeded south to what is now the Churchill River in Saskatchewan, and returned to Denmark after braving a bitter winter.

Another Danish explorer, Vitus Jonassen Bering (1681–1741), sailed under the Russian flag. Bering led a series of expeditions eastward from Russia and across the north Pacific to the northwest coast of America. He discovered the Bering Strait in 1728 and Alaska in 1741. He also found the Aleutian Islands off the Alaskan coast. Bering died on an uninhabited island in the southwest of what is now called the Bering Sea.

Danish Colonists

Because Holland and Denmark had enjoyed close relations for centuries, in the 17th century, Dutch merchants, familiar with Denmark's reputation as a seafaring nation, hired Danish sailors to man their vessels. Holland also enlisted Danes to inhabit settlements managed by the Dutch West India Company for the purpose of opening additional trade markets.

In the 1620s, Danes joined the Dutch in New Amsterdam (now New York). The first Danish immigrant

In the 1620s, many Danes helped settle the Dutch colony of New Amsterdam—modern-day Manhattan, the heart of New York City.

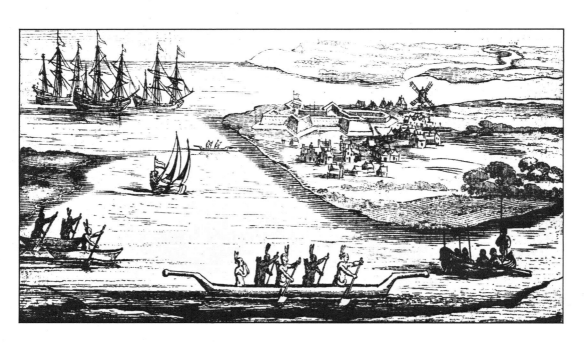

Eighteenth-century Moravian Pietists attend a marriage ceremony before embarking for America, which promised them religious freedom.

family, headed by Jan Jansen, reached America in 1636, but they changed their name to Van Breestede to fit in better with their fellow settlers. By 1675, about a hundred Danes had arrived, including Jonas Bronck, who purchased a 500-acre stretch of land along the Hudson River in New York from local Indians. Today, this site is included in the New York City borough that bears Bronck's name: the Bronx. Bronck's friend and brother-in-law, Jochem Pietersen Kuyter, became the first European to settle in Manhattan, on the northern end of the island.

In 1735, Denmark became embroiled in religious strife. Moravian Pietism, a branch of Protestantism that emphasized personal Bible study, won a following among some Danes. The Lutheran church, threatened by the new sect, outlawed it, and the dissenters looked to America for religious freedom. They joined their German coreligionists in Bethlehem, Pennsylvania, where a bell made by Danish craftsman Mathias Tammerup is still rung today. Once again, the Danes found themselves an ethnic minority, and they assimilated so quickly into the German community that it is difficult to estimate their numbers.

In the 18th century, Danes colonized the Caribbean island of St. Croix.

During this period, the Danish West Indies Company acquired the Caribbean island of St. Thomas. The company struggled financially, even with the assistance of slaves imported from Guinea. In 1754, the crown took over the island and opened it to all Danish citizens. Settlers moved onto the island of St. John, and later to St. Croix when it was purchased from France. The region eventually boasted flourishing plantations where tobacco, sugar, and cotton were grown. In 1917, Denmark sold these islands to the United States, and they became the U.S. Virgin Islands.

During the 17th century, Great Britain also had begun to colonize the New World, and its English settlers enjoyed close relations with the Danish West Indies. Well-to-do Danish planters sent their children to the American mainland, especially Philadelphia, to be educated. A number of Danes, moreover, migrated from the islands to America.

Later, Danes from the West Indies joined the American Revolution. Hans Christian Febiger (1749–1796) became one of George Washington's most trusted officers. Known to his men as "Old Denmark," Febiger fought valiantly in the battles of Bunker Hill and Brandywine. In 1783, Congress awarded him the rank of brigadier general. He later was elected Pennsylvania's state treasurer.

Danes on the Frontier

Danish immigration picked up during the first half of the 19th century, but the number of newcomers remained small. Most were artisans, adventurers, and professionals who settled in cities, especially New York. Unmarried when they arrived to make their fortunes, they usually wed women born in America and easily blended into the mainstream. This pattern of marrying outside the group distinguishes Danish immigrants from others. Asians, for example, summoned brides from their homeland, and Eastern European immigrants often journeyed home to search for suitable brides.

Some Danes, however, chose not to remain in East Coast cities and instead ventured into the plains and the wilderness of the American West. One such pioneer was

This sketch of the pioneer group led by Peter Lassen (sleeping against the tree) was drawn by one of its members.

Peter Lassen (1800–1859), a blacksmith who sailed from Denmark to Boston in 1830, then led a group of homesteaders across the Rocky Mountains and into California. Lassen's ambition was to find gold. He turned up little of the precious ore but helped blaze the trail used later in the great gold rush of 1849. Lassen Peak and California's Lassen Volcanic National Park are named in his honor.

Another Danish American who headed west was Charles Zanco (1808–1836), an immigrant from Randers, Denmark, who died at the famous battle of the Alamo in San Antonio. He fought the Mexicans alongside such frontier heroes as Davy Crockett and Jim Bowie. Little is known about Zanco, but some scholars credit him with designing an early version of Texas's "Lone Star" flag.

An equally valiant Danish American was Christian Linde. Born in 1817 to a noble Danish family in Copenhagen, Linde was educated in medicine at the Royal University of Copenhagen. He immigrated to America

Danish American Charles Zanco died at the Alamo in 1836.

in 1884 and headed for Oshkosh, Wisconsin. Soon, he became a respected doctor who tended European settlers and also native Americans, who called him "Muckwa" (white bear) because he was large and had blond hair. Linde wrote a number of articles and books about surgery, and his achievements had won him a national reputation by the time of his death in 1887.

The population of Danish immigrants included peasants lured to North America by the promise of arable farmland.

The Great Migration

Between 1867 and 1914 almost 300,000 Danes came to the United States and Canada, a small number compared to the several million immigrants who came from Ireland, Germany, and Sweden. Still, this migration was a 20-fold increase over the total population that previously migrated to the New World. Moreover, by 1900, the children of these immigrants already outnumbered their parents.

The mass emigration from Denmark occurred late because of steadily improving political and social conditions in the homeland. In 1849, for example, a liberal constitution went into effect, expanding the personal freedom of Denmark's citizens. There was cultural progress, too, marked by the advent of compulsory education and a flowering of literature and the arts. During this time, Denmark gave the world not only Hans Christian Andersen, but philosopher Søren Kierke-

gaard (1813–1855), sculptor Bertel Thorvaldsen (1770–1844), and painter Christen Kobke (1810–1898).

At the same time, the population in Denmark was starting to soar, straining the labor market, which was flooded with new workers. Unemployment grew and with it came increased poverty. Many landless peasants, forced to leave the countryside, sought job opportunities in the factories that were springing up in Copenhagen and other urban areas. But the factories could not employ enough workers to quell the crisis, and those desperate for jobs often set sail for the New World. On top of these problems, in 1864 Denmark suffered a humiliating military defeat at the hands of Prussia and was forced to surrender almost one-fourth of its territory. Approximately 50,000 Danish-speaking people left the conquered provinces, and the majority migrated to America. Finally, a conservative government emerged that reversed previous reforms and curtailed many of the freedoms Danes had come to enjoy.

All this activity hastened and swelled the tide of Danish immigration to North America, although not everyone who came was a victim of Denmark's shifting political and social alignment. America represented a fresh start, and many people felt drawn to the young nation for highly personal reasons: a bad love affair, family disagreements, wanderlust, or a desire to escape the past. Prisoners, for instance, sometimes left Denmark after being released from jail. One such immigrant wrote:

> What can the former convict do in Denmark? Work? Impossible! . . . He who comes over here . . . has no funds, no family from whom he can freeload, but has to work simply to keep alive. To his surprise, he realizes that only the first step hurts, and that he earns twice as much as in Denmark. Suddenly . . . things begin to fall into place. . . . The old saying is true, that "I don't care what you have been, but rather what you are."

Immigrants board a steamer bound for New York in the 1890s.

Most immigrants of this period were young men, 55 percent of them between the ages of 15 and 29. The vast majority were rural peasants and farmers. Industrial and domestic workers formed the second largest group, and artisans, including smiths, bricklayers, carpenters, and bakers, the third. Handmade goods had lost markets dominated by cheaper mass-produced factory items, and craftworkers were faced with the choice of giving up their livelihoods or plying their trade in America.

Most rural laborers immigrating to America hoped to own their own farms. The Homestead Act of 1862, one of the most important stimuli to European immigration, made this aspiration a possibility by stating that anyone over the age of 21 who did not own land elsewhere could claim 160 acres of unoccupied government land in the unsettled regions of the United States. Homesteaders had to agree to certain stipulations, for instance, that they live on the property and not put it up for sale. However, after five years, the settler was given the deed to the land. The act was so successful that in 1872 Canada introduced a similar law, the Dominion Land Act. For many of Denmark's land-starved farmers, these acts were a lifeline, and a welcome opportunity to start life anew in North America.

A crew member searches for stowaways in the crowded steerage bunks.

Religious Minorities

There was yet another reason why many Danes left their homeland: religious persecution. Though the vast majority of Denmark's population belonged to the Lutheran church, the state's official faith, religious minorities also existed and, at times, suffered oppression. The Moravians, who came to Pennsylvania in the mid-1700s, were one such dissident sect. A century later, missionaries from the United States went to Denmark and converted significant numbers to newer Protestant faiths, such as Baptism and Mormonism. These converts eventually found Denmark inhospitable. In 1839, for instance, Baptist missionaries from the United States organized their first congregation in Denmark; they were soon harassed by Lutheran officials who arranged for the imprisonment of Baptist leaders. In 1854, organized emigration of Baptists from Denmark began.

The largest religious minority to emigrate from Denmark were members of the Church of Jesus Christ of Latter-day Saints, or Mormons. Mormon missionaries arrived in Denmark from Utah in 1850 and by the

Thingvalla—the first Danish line to send steamships across the Atlantic—advertised its fares in Copenhagen newspapers.

This building in Vejle, on the Jutland peninsula, housed the Direct Hamburg-American Emigration Company, which sold steamship tickets to Danish immigrants.

end of the century they had baptized more than 20,000 converts. Mormon doctrines—particularly the practice of polygamy, whereby one man took several wives—caused great controversy in Denmark. Mormons were denounced from the Lutheran pulpit and were vilified in church publications.

This persecution, together with the Mormon teaching that its members should gather in the "Zion" of Utah, led more than half of Denmark's converts to immigrate under the auspices of the Mormon church, which supervised the details of their passage, chartering ships and arranging the long overland trek from New York harbor to Utah. Those who could not afford tickets for the transatlantic voyage could borrow money from a church fund. From 1860 to 1870, Utah had the largest Danish population in the American territories.

The Transatlantic Journey

Before the advent of the steamship in the 1860s, immigrants had to make the arduous journey on sailing vessels that were designed primarily for carrying wheat and cotton. The Atlantic crossing took from four to five weeks, and the poorer immigrants were crowded into steerage without fresh food or proper sanitary conditions. There were frequent burials at sea, as many died of diseases such as typhoid fever, cholera, and smallpox. As one steerage passenger wrote to his family:

> This was the most unpleasant journey I have ever made. The sea was almost always rough, and it wasn't safe to go up on the deck. I fell down only once, but some of the other passengers fell about three times a day. It was impossible to stay down below very long because of the lice and stench, but it was also impossible to stand on the deck without being drenched in an hour.

Though the use of steampower shortened the trip to about 10 days, conditions on board were still often deplorable. As before, the boats were cramped, food was terrible, and passengers sometimes pilfered one another's luggage. And Danes, products of a society where almost everyone belonged to the same race and religion, often felt uncomfortable in the company of the different ethnic groups on board with them.

Things improved in 1879, when Denmark acquired its first steamship line, the *Thingvalla*, which sailed directly from Copenhagen to New York. One satisfied passenger, writing to a Danish newspaper, commended

In order to swell its passenger lists, the Illinois Central Railroad offered tracts of land to pioneers.

the ship and its crew, singling out the cook, baker, and menu for special praise. This passenger enthusiastically described a "two-course lunch with fresh cakes (we had apples only once; that was on a stormy day)" and a dinner with "lobster, sardines, aquavit, anchovies, tea, and so on. Everything was served in generous, well-prepared portions."

Arriving in Force

In the early 1800s, Danish migration was fueled by descriptions of life in America sent home in immigrant letters and published regularly in local newspapers. This correspondence expressed a wide range of opinions about conditions in the New World. Some newcomers felt America was inhospitable, even lawless, but most were optimistic. So many Danes were intrigued by the prospect of the New World that in 1847 the first guidebook for Danish immigrants was published.

Further incentives were supplied by active publicists for the New World. One such was Rasmus Sørenson (1799–1865), a radical politician who advocated land reform and education for Danish peasants. Disillusioned with Denmark's lack of commitment to the poor, he encouraged them to emigrate and published a series of articles based on letters sent from his son, who had made a fresh start in Wisconsin. Sørenson visited

(continued on page 57)

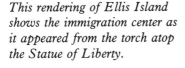

This rendering of Ellis Island shows the immigration center as it appeared from the torch atop the Statue of Liberty.

OLD
MEETS
NEW

*Contemporary Denmark contains many reminders of the nation's storied past.
On the Faeroe Islands, far north of the mainland, young Danes wearing
traditional garb pose by a harbor, and a mother and her children relax on an
old farm. A horse-drawn beer wagon adds a nostalgic touch to a bustling
street in Denmark's capital, Copenhagen.*

In Edvard Petersen's 1890 painting Departure from Larsens Plads *emigrants prepare to board a ship headed for North America.*

53

Founded in 1910, Solvang, California, provides a vision of old Denmark, especially during "Danish Days," an annual festival held in September and visited by thousands of tourists.

The fairy tales of Hans Christian Andersen have delighted millions of readers throughout the world. This statue of Andersen adorns Tivoli Square in Solvang.

(continued from page 48)

there himself in 1852, returned to Denmark in the 1860s to lecture on the United States and lead groups of Danes to the New World.

Another radical who aided immigrant groups was Mogens Abraham Sommer (1829–1901). Jailed several times in Denmark for his attacks on the king and clergy, Sommer immigrated to New York in 1861, but soon returned to Denmark and opened an emigration office in Copenhagen. He escorted groups of immigrants to Wisconsin and Chicago, crossing the Atlantic thirteen times.

After the 1870s, immigration agents became commonplace in Denmark. Some agents worked for American railroad companies that were anxious to find farmers who were willing to buy surplus land granted to these companies by the government in order to lessen the cost of building new tracks. If companies sold the surplus, they profited twice: first from the land sale, then from the goods transported along their routes by the farmers.

American steamship lines recruited immigrants in order to swell passenger lists. Company agents established offices in Danish cities and then contracted operatives throughout the country; they sold tickets as a sideline and collected high commissions. In this way, even the inhabitants of tiny, out-of-the-way villages learned of transportation possibilities to America. The

In the early 1900s, immigrants lined up for medical examinations at Ellis Island.

Many Danish immigrants settled in Wither, Wisconsin, in the late 19th century.

agents sometimes helped find jobs for immigrants and often proved an invaluable source of information about life in the New World. Agents also established offices in America and were visited by Danish Americans who sent prepaid steamer tickets to their relatives in Denmark. In the last quarter of the 19th century, one-quarter of all immigrants traveled with such prepaid tickets.

Entering America

In the late 19th century, millions of immigrants from all over Europe arrived in New York harbor. Before they could begin new lives in America, they had to pass through an immigrant station: Castle Garden until 1892, and, thereafter, Ellis Island. At these stations newcomers submitted to medical inspections meant to root out contagious diseases, such as typhus and cholera, which some immigrants carried on board with them. The inspection could be humiliating, especially for women whose skirts were roughly pulled up in full public view. Further degradations were in store as men, women, and children were poked and prodded, an experience so harrowing that Ellis Island became known as the "Isle of Tears."

One immigrant from Denmark, Marie Christensen, recounted her childhood experiences for a Danish-American magazine. Marie was eight years old in 1904 when she arrived in New York with her mother, brother, and two sisters. They had been preceded two years earlier by Marie's father, who, like most male immigrants, wanted to get a secure financial footing before sending for his family. During the two-week voyage Marie and the others suffered violent seasickness, but they had all recovered by the time they passed the Statue of Liberty and docked at Ellis Island.

Upon arrival in New York, the first- and second-class passengers remained on board, where they were quickly checked by doctors and sent on their way. But poor travelers, such as Marie and her family, were relegated to third-class quarters where unsanitary conditions often exposed passengers to contagious diseases. Physicians subjected these passengers to difficult and sometimes painful examinations. Marie heard her mother scream as a doctor lifted her eyelids with an

In 1908, Danish Americans gather outside the Lutheran church in Danevang, Texas, a community that sought to preserve Old World ethnicity.

instrument that looked like a buttonhook. Had he found traces of trachoma, a contagious eye infection, Marie's mother would never have been able to enter America.

The Christensens then underwent further inspections. Mrs. Christensen was grilled by customs officials. How had the family paid for their passage across the Atlantic? How old were they all? Were they anarchists—political revolutionaries—bent on overthrowing the United States government? Mrs. Christensen, who spoke no English, failed to understand these questions, and no one could come to her aid: not one official on Ellis island spoke Danish and the passenger list included no other Danish-speakers besides the Christensens. Fortunately, the customs official who interviewed Mrs. Christensen found her trustworthy, and the family was permitted to pass to the final inspection station.

There, the Christensens' luck ran out. An entry fee was required of all immigrants. Mrs. Christensen was willing to pay it, but her money had been stolen during the journey. She had thought she could send a telegram to her husband requesting funds, but that, too, cost more than she could afford. The family was forced to wait two weeks and got lost in the shuffle among the huge numbers of immigrants—more than 30,000 were processed at Ellis Island each week, and officials gave their attention to the numerous eastern and southern European immigrants rather than to Scandinavians. Finally, someone had the good sense to call in the Danish Consulate, which arranged for Mrs. Christensen to send her telegram. Two days later, they received the money and left to join Mr. Christensen in Akron, Ohio.

Where Danes Settled

After passing through Ellis Island, many Danish immigrants promptly headed to the Midwest and its vast tracts of farmland, made available by the Homestead Act. The region was especially appealing to Danes be-

Danish Americans helped settle Partridge, Minnesota, in the early 1900s.

In 1908 Christian and Kirsten Madsen posed for this photograph on their Danevang homestead.

cause its terrain resembled their homeland and seemed ideal for the dairy farming they had practiced in Denmark for generations.

Until the mid-19th century, there were not enough Danes in the frontier to form their own communities, so they often lived alongside other ethnic groups, particularly Norwegians. In 1846 the first Danish-American settlement was founded, in Hartland, Wisconsin. This state attracted many Danes, who populated numerous parts of it, even establishing the town of New Denmark. The larger city of Racine, first settled in 1839, still retains a strong Danish flavor. By 1900, almost 3,000 Danes lived there, and today, half of Racine's 85,000 residents are of Danish descent.

From Wisconsin, some Danish immigrants proceeded to Iowa and its rich soil. In 1865, Elk Horn was founded, and it developed into a cohesive Danish-American community. It had a Danish school, a Lutheran church, and an orphanage. The immigrants also organized cooperatives that provided insurance, lumber, and dairy products. The preferred language was Danish, even for children. In 1986, the first Danish Immigrant Museum was opened in Elk Horn, and it houses a permanent collection of immigrant artifacts and letters.

A Danish flag marks the Peterson farm, also in Danevang.

Most Danes inhabited heterogeneous communities, a situation that some found distressing. Between 1886 and 1935, Danish leaders attempted to preserve Danish ethnicity by establishing rural settlements in various locations. The Dansk Folkesamfund (Danish Folk Society) arranged for arable land to be sold only to Danes with the provision that they stay on it for a fixed number of years. Among such settlements were Tyler and Askov (both in Minnesota); Danevang, Texas; Dagmar, Montana; and Solvang, California.

These far-flung communities are evidence that although Danes usually chose to live in the Midwest, many lit out for distant regions. As early as 1860, the largest number of representatives of the group lived in Utah, the state founded by the Mormon church. And Danes have inhabited every American state and territory since 1870. In that year, Wisconsin had the highest population of Danish Americans. Between 1890 and 1920, Iowa's population surpassed it. Minnesota ranked third. Even so, in 1910 more than 70 percent of Danish-born Americans lived outside these three Midwestern states. In 1920, California became the state with the most Danish-Americans and remains so to this day.

Danes also established neighborhoods in urban areas, particularly Chicago, which until the 1930s had the largest urban concentration of Danes outside Denmark. Other neighborhoods developed in New York and in Minnesota's Twin Cities, Minneapolis and St. Paul.

Danish Americans discovered that the ups and downs of urban experience differed sharply from the stability of the farm. Some Danes complained of unemployment, bad housing, and low wages, others of bigotry, perpetuated by more established immigrant groups. Yet, many immigrants responded to the energy and technological wonders of America's urban centers. One newcomer who took up residence in Chicago wrote, "Here in the capital city of the cities there is a lot to see. The courthouse is a real palace of marble and sandstone. Christiansborg Palace in Copenhagen is only a shadow of it in size and magnificence."

Gradually, Danish Americans evolved a taste for city life and the group's population filtered away from the farm. In the 1970s, a century after the major immigration wave, at least 80 percent of Danish Americans lived in urban areas, with the largest concentration in Chicago and Los Angeles. A scant 4 percent still live on farms.

Danes in Canada

Of the early Danish immigrants who landed in North America between 1869 and 1914 only 5 percent headed directly to Canada. Before long, however, some of the remaining 95 percent migrated north to Canada's prairies. One popular destination was the province of Alberta. An attempt was made there to establish Danish as the official language, although the majority of the community had already switched to English during their stay in the United States. As a group, Danish Canadians, like Danish Americans, were less interested in retaining their native heritage than in clearing land and building farms.

Danish immigration to Canada increased between 1921 and 1931, primarily because the United States established restrictive quotas, limiting immigration on a nation-by-nation basis. During this period, more than 30 percent of all Danish immigrants to the New World made Canada their home. ✎

Danish Americans, dressed in their summer clothes, ride out for the day from Danevang, Texas.

LIFE IN AMERICA

Many Danes found their new homeland exciting and full of promise, but for others America fell short of their expectations. It was a constant struggle to survive on the frontier: living conditions usually were primitive; winters could be brutal; the work of clearing land and planting crops was backbreaking. And once their strenuous efforts were over, farmers often were victimized by unpredictable business cycles. In the 1890s, for example, many farmers were wiped out when a drastic drop in grain prices made it impossible for them to pay their bills.

Letters from the New World

Many immigrants recorded their observations of America in letters sent to family, friends, and hometown newspapers in Denmark. Translated and collected in *Danes in North America*, a book published in 1984, this correspondence enables contemporary readers to glimpse the complex adjustments Danes made to the New World.

One settler described the primitive conditions of his new home, Texas: "Yesterday I took a drive to exercise my two horses, but in some places the mud was so deep they sank in up to their stomachs. . . . The small farmers here are, on the whole, in poor shape; they usually don't produce enough to pay their hired hands, if they have any. Usually they do most of the work themselves."

These formally attired Danish Americans play croquet, a favorite pastime among well-bred Europeans.

A striking contrast is offered by a Missouri field-worker, who marveled at the richness of the soil: "The fields here are very hilly, and there is a lot of forested land. All in all, the soil is the best that can be found. We plowed the land immediately and planted corn in it. The first year the grain is the best you can imagine." And yet another view was given by a farmer in Washington State: "What Washington demands is a hardy, patient farmer who is willing to clear the forest and till the soil for many years and expect nothing more than his daily bread. Only in the distant future will he, or more correctly, his descendants, be able to reap the fruits of seven years' arduous labor."

Danes were accustomed to cold Scandinavian winters, but many found the long Canadian winters more punishing than anything in their experience. "We are waiting for spring here, but it still hasn't arrived," wrote a woman in New Brunswick, the Canadian province adjacent to the state of Maine. "It is disgustingly cold. I can stand it in the winter, but at this time of year it is just crazy." Another woman gave a poetic description of the landscape in the western province of Saskatchewan: "The wild prairie seems so barren and strange. It's like a sea. We are just a speck in the middle of a circle that grows or shrinks as the weather changes."

Urban conditions elicited an entirely different set of reactions from Danish immigrants. One correspondent was distressed by the large numbers of unemployed people in Chicago: "The most pitiful sight are the many fathers, some fairly old, who come over here with wives and children, often nearly penniless. As soon as they arrive in this unknown, partly lawless country whose language they do not understand, they are surrounded by thousands of scoundrels who are only conniving to deceive them and cheat them out of their money and clothing."

But another immigrant found Chicago so inviting that he encouraged a friend in Denmark to join him there: "I have often thought that America really is the place for you, my friend. I know from experience, as you do, how hard it often is to get by back home. But here everyone who wants to work does far better. You are a carpenter by trade, and here in Chicago there are

In the early 1900s, Jensen's Creamery employed many Danish-American Mormons in Salt Lake City, Utah.

eight thousand carpenters working under very favorable conditions."

The Ethnic Smorgasbord

Among the novelties Danish immigrants discovered in American cities was the array of ethnic groups. Sometimes their encounters with them had unpleasant consequences. Denmark, after all, was a homogeneous society—almost everyone belonged to the same race and religion. Thus, many Danes were bemused by the customs and habits of immigrants from different backgrounds. A Danish American, describing the Chinatown in Portland, wrote: "Their buildings are decorated with a large jumble of Chinese characters and ornamented with some gadgets that by American standards seem bizarre."

Some of these prejudices stemmed from long-standing political conflicts that originated in troubled international relations in Europe. Germans, for instance, were especially resented because they conquered Dan-

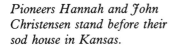

Pioneers Hannah and John Christensen stand before their sod house in Kansas.

Danish-American garment workers crowd into a sweatshop in Racine, Wisconsin. In the 1980s, half the city's population traced its lineage back to Denmark.

ish territory in the 19th century. One letter written from St. Louis accused German Americans of importing their homeland's expansionist ways: "In the mayoral election in St. Louis last Monday the Germans did everything they could to elect their candidate. Fortunately, he was defeated." Some Danish Americans even looked askance at Swedes, a perception grounded in the two countries' ancient rivalry for control of northern Europe.

Objectionable as these attitudes seem today, they help illustrate the rawness of 19th-century America, a place where strangers from sharply divergent, different cultures vied for a share of the promised land. Because Danes settled in all parts of the country and lived alongside people from many different nationalities, they gained a unique vantage point for surveying the bewildering variety of American life. Their letters to Denmark reflect all the frustrations and pleasures involved in carving a place in this emerging society.

Chicago-Posten, *a Danish-language weekly, helped newcomers adapt to the New World and stay in touch with their homeland.*

Fitting In

Though some Danes felt at odds with other ethnic groups, they blended very quickly into the American mainstream. Thanks to their high literacy rate, Danes usually learned English swiftly. As early as 1883, Danes had their first English-language journal, *Scandinavia.* By 1911, 97 percent of all Danish immigrants employed in mining and manufacturing spoke English, compared with 53 percent of the other immigrants who had been in the country for the same time. By 1930, 75 percent of the 180,000 Danish immigrants had become naturalized citizens.

Their rapid mastery of English, however, was not the only reason why the group assimilated so easily. Another reason was that many Danes had forsaken their homeland at a time when nationalistic feelings had plummeted among the entire population. Denmark had suffered a humiliating military defeat by Germany and was forced to surrender much of the southern Jutland peninsula. Many inhabitants in the conquered territories grew disenchanted with the Danish government and quickly emigrated to North America. When they arrived, they were eager to shed their old national identity and take on a new one.

In addition, most Danes came to America for economic reasons, and fitting into the mainstream ensured greater financial rewards than holding on to their Danish identity. As one immigrant noted: "The Danes I knew didn't want to speak Danish anymore—we wanted to speak English. Danish wasn't going to get us anywhere in America." Once they gained a footing in America, many Danish immigrants married spouses outside their own ethnic population, mainly because there were so few eligible women immigrants. Mixed marriages naturally speeded up the assimilation process.

A major reason that Danish Americans were accepted by other Americans was the willingness of Danish immigrants to sever their traditional Lutheran affiliations, unlike other newcomers who clung to their ancestral religions. Immigrants from Ireland and Italy, for example, held fast to their Catholic identity, those from Greece formed congregations that kept alive the

The interior of this Lutheran church, located near Cozad, Nebraska, resembles the much older places of worship attended by Danes in their homeland.

elaborate rites of Eastern Orthodoxy, and devout Jews from Eastern Europe worshiped in synagogues wherever they settled. Danish immigrants were a startling exception. Most either joined no American church or rejected Lutheranism for a more established Protestant sect, such as the Baptist churches, Methodism, or Mormonism. This trend was so pronounced that by 1920 only about 9 percent of the Danish-American community belonged to the Danish Lutheran church.

Another major factor in the relatively painless acclimation of Danish immigrants was race. Like the powerful "Yankees" who constituted America's ruling class, Danes were white and descended from the so-called Nordic, or North European, people. As a result, they were spared the racism directed at African Americans, Chinese Americans, and at immigrants from Southern and Eastern Europe. Seldom perceived as a threat by more established Americans, Danish immigrants generally were accepted throughout the United States.

Twentieth-Century Immigration

After 1921, the United States instituted a quota system limiting immigration from all nations, including Denmark. Three years later another law was passed that placed the total number of immigrants at 150,000; this

A classic small-town courting scene: A Danish-American couple poses outside a Utah hotel in the early 20th century.

total was then broken down on a country by country basis, depending on the percentage of the existing U.S. population that already claimed ancestry from different nations. The law thus favored groups that had secured a foothold in America and was designed to bar new ethnic groups from entering the country. Though Danish Americans were an established ethnic group, they still were affected by the immigration crackdown and responded as other groups did—by aiming their sights at Canada. During this period, more than 38 percent of all Danish immigrants to the New World made Canada their home.

In the next decade—the 1930s—Danish immigration to the United States was reduced further by the Great Depression, which damaged the American economy, and did not pick up again until after World War II. It soon leveled off to approximately 1,000 new arrivals per year. Canada, by contrast, remained a haven for Danish immigrants. Between 1955 and 1960 Canada took in more Danish immigrants than any other country in the world. In 1957 alone, Canada received more than 7,000 Danes. The Canadian census of 1981 records 90,000 Canadians of Danish origin, many of them living in the far western provinces of British Columbia and Alberta. ✎

Danish Americans often gathered at social centers and saloons such as Lagoni's in Chicago, pictured in this 1898 photograph.

In 1853, Claus L. Clausen founded the Norwegian Evangelical Lutheran church in America.

THE DANISH-AMERICAN COMMUNITY

For many American ethnic groups the focus of the community has been the church. An Eastern European people such as the Slovaks, for example, often did not consider themselves truly settled in the New World until they had built an Orthodox church where they could observe services and also mingle with other members of the community. Groups such as Irish Americans and Italian Americans found sanctuary from anti-Catholicism behind the walls of churches where they met for religious and social events.

Americans of Danish descent placed less emphasis on churchgoing, mainly because religion had been less important in their homeland. Ninety-seven percent of all Danes were born into Lutheranism, Denmark's state religion, but relatively few citizens felt a strong allegiance to it. Moreover, the church was split into two dissenting factions whose heated conflicts resurfaced in America. Many Danes lost faith in a religion that seemed more concerned with finger-pointing than with spiritual leadership.

Churches

Unlike Denmark, America has no state religion. Churches receive no government subsidies and depend for their survival on the financial offerings made by individual worshipers. Few immigrants, however, were willing or able to meet this expense. Thus, it has been estimated that only 35 percent of all Danish Americans belonged to a church. Even so, there were a number of strong Danish Lutheran congregations, especially in rural areas where they also served as social centers of the community.

Danish Americans who wished to preserve their national Lutheran heritage began to worship together in the 1870s. Before then, the immigrant population was so small and scattered that few Danish-American communities were large enough to support their own church, and most of their inhabitants joined Lutheran congregations established by Norwegian, Swedish, or German immigrants.

A number of these mixed congregations were led by Danish pastors, such as Claus L. Clausen, who in 1853 founded the Norwegian Evangelical Lutheran Church in America. Clausen's influence was wide-ranging. He helped start settlements and congregations throughout Iowa, served in Iowa state offices, and was the first

Danish Americans wear traditional garb at an ethnic festival in Askov, Minnesota, a community formed along the philosophical lines of N. F. S. Grundtvig.

Members of a Nebraska Lutheran church pose for a photographer as part of a celebration held on the first Sunday following Easter, 1912.

president of the Norwegian-Danish Lutheran conference. In addition, Clausen traveled to Denmark and encouraged religious leaders to send pastors to America. Two years later, the Danish State Church established the "Commission for the Furtherance of the Proclamation of the Gospel among Danes in America." This commission sent four pastors to the United States, and in 1872 they founded the American Danish Lutheran Church.

Internal discord kept Danish Lutheran churches from becoming a cohesive force in the community. The divisions, or schisms, traced back to the old country. There, in the 1860s, the state Lutheran church split into two factions. Repercussions soon were felt in America, where one Lutheran sect, known as the Danish Evangelical Lutheran Church, or Danish Church, followed the teachings of the Danish pastor N. F. S. Grundtvig. Nicknamed the "Happy Danes," they emphasized the importance of joy in Christian life and also the preservation of Danish cultural identity. They encouraged Danish Americans to speak Danish and to continue customs practiced in the homeland. Active in the United States, the Danish Church founded schools, a seminary in West Denmark, Wisconsin, and Grand View College in Des Moines, Iowa. In 1962 this church merged with three other denominations to become the Lutheran Church in America.

In 1894, the Inner Mission Society—or "Holy Danes"—founded Trinity Seminar in Blair, Nebraska. This photograph shows its faculty.

The other Danish Lutheran denomination was the Inner Mission Society, nicknamed the "Holy Danes." They believed in a literal interpretation of the Bible, strict morality in daily life, and in Christian fellowship. They also worked to convert others to their faith, often through fiery revival meetings at which pastors preached repentance and church members publicly recounted their spiritual experiences.

Followers of this sect argued against preservation of the Danish heritage. They wanted to Americanize quickly, using the English language to spread the Gospel. This group formally became the United Evangelical Lutheran church in 1894, and in that same year established Trinity Seminary and Dana College, both in Blair, Nebraska. Thereafter, it was known as the Blair church. In 1962, it merged with the Lutheran Church in America.

These two major factions opposed each other on many theological and cultural issues, and their disagreements were compounded by personal feuds between pastors. A formal schism occurred in 1894 and lasted into the 1920s, causing many Danish communities to build two separate churches to house the rival factions. Ultimately, the controversy lessened the role of the Danish-American church. Instead of becoming a focal point for communities, churches often became a divisive influence on those who wanted to remain in the fold.

The first Danish Lutheran churches in America were founded in the 1870s. Before then, and before the acrimonious split in church leadership, some Danes turned to other forms of Protestantism, chiefly the Baptist churches and Methodism. The earliest Danish-language Baptist church was founded in Potter County, Pennsylvania in 1854. Within a decade, there were 10 Danish Baptist congregations in the Midwest, all organized by Lars Jørgensen Hauge. The Baptist religion was also growing in the Norwegian community, and church membership included worshipers of both nationalities. In 1864 a Danish-Norwegian Baptist Conference promoted cooperation between descendants of the two Scandinavian countries.

These congregations shared the same values as English-speaking Baptist sects. Like them, Danish Baptists believed in strong church discipline and strict adherence to the Sabbath, which meant that drinking alcohol, among other indulgences, was prohibited. Though the total number of Danish Baptists had reached only about 5,000 by 1909, the church figured prominently in their lives, not least by forcing many Danish immigrants to learn English so that they could participate in religious services.

Like Baptist churches, Methodist churches often included Norwegian and Danish worshipers. The first congregation of Scandinavian-American Methodists was founded in 1856 in Cambridge, Wisconsin, by Christian B. Willerup. He returned to Europe in 1856 and became a missionary in Norway and Denmark. In the United States, Scandinavian Methodists, again like their Baptist counterparts, formed a separate subgroup of the larger English-speaking Methodist body until they became fully integrated into it in 1943. Before the merger, Danish Methodists numbered only a few thousand.

The American church that gained the biggest number of Danish-American converts was the Church of Jesus Christ of the Latter-day Saints, or Mormons. In the 1850s, the church sent missionaries to Denmark who made many successful conversions. The Mormon leadership was anxious to bolster its community and thus encouraged converts to leave their homelands for Utah, where the church was headquartered. Many Danes risked the journey, spurred on by hostility in Denmark. In fact, the first significant wave of Danish immigrants to the United States were Mormons, and between 1850 and 1905 more than 12,000 Danish Mormons came to the New World.

Every aspect of the Mormon migration was thoroughly planned. Well-organized wagon trains crossed the Midwestern prairies and continued on to Utah. By the time passengers reached "Zion," they were already used to working in highly disciplined groups. As a result, most Danish Mormons integrated quickly into the larger Mormon community. At first, the newcomers attended their own special meetings for religious instruction, plays, and social events, and they read a Danish-language newspaper, *Bikuben* (The Beehive). But eventually they gave up most aspects of Danish culture.

The Mormon influx lessened in the 1870s as the number of conversions in Europe decreased. Social and political conditions had improved in Denmark and fewer citizens looked to the Mormon church for the promise of a better life. At the same time, the American Mormon community in Utah had grown to a satisfactory size and the leadership felt less driven to add to its membership.

Folk Schools

Probably the most remarkable contribution that Danish immigrants made to America was the folk high school. Founded in the middle of the 19th century, Danish folk schools were based on the philosophies of N. F. S. Grundtvig, a bishop and member of Denmark's Parlia-

By the time Danish Mormons reached Utah, they had already become a well-organized and tightly knit community. This wagon train was photographed in 1879.

The only Danish-American folk school still in existence is Danebod in Tyler, Minnesota. This photograph of the school's dormitory—flying the Danish flag—dates from 1900.

ment who fought for the rights of farmers and for a political democracy based on free adult education. A social reformer with firm beliefs, Grundtvig argued that education should include not only the accumulation of knowledge, but also character development. Grundtvig's movement further stressed the appreciation of Danish culture. Folk schools founded on Grundtvig's principles had no entrance requirements, no exams, and no diplomas. Students and teachers treated one another as equals, often living in the same building and sharing meals.

The first Danish immigrants, who brought with them many values learned from Grundtvig, transplanted folk schools on to American soil, where they grew to become centers of a large progressive movement that affected entire communities. Towns began to hold educational public meetings and to erect community halls. Another outgrowth of this movement was the formation, in 1870, of the United Farmer's party, a political organization dedicated to helping ordinary citizens gain a collective voice. Political participation came naturally to immigrants from Denmark because of their strong education and background in political democracy.

In America, virtually every Danish folk school was founded by leaders of the Danish Lutheran Church. In an atmosphere of religious devotion, pupils studied the Danish language; the histories of Denmark, America, and the church; mathematics; penmanship; Danish and American literature; Swedish gymnastics and folk-dancing, along with singing and various group activities. Students learned mostly through lectures, though some books were available.

The folk school movement had detractors. The evangelical membership of the Inner Mission, for example, found the curriculum too secular and thought a stronger effort should be made to guide students toward specific religious beliefs. An altogether different set of objections was raised by those who believed the schools should be a carbon copy of the original Danish institutions instead of being modified to fit more easily into an American setting. These "purists" insisted that the main goals of the schools should be spiritual rather than academic or vocational. Eventually, however, folk schools such as the one in Elk Horn, Iowa (America's first, opened in 1878), altered the traditional focus by

Danebod's original curriculum included rigorous physical education, as shown in this photograph of the school's gym.

introducing business courses, teacher training, and a college preparatory program. Despite some protests, enrollment increased after these more practical courses were added.

Gradually, a shortage of folk school funds and the growth of the American education system took its toll, and the movement faltered. The last school was founded in Dalum, Canada, in 1921. Today, Danebod, in Tyler, Minnesota, is the only folk school still in existence, and its buildings mainly serve the community at large as a setting for conferences and summer camps. It is estimated that a total of only 10,000 to 12,000 students ever attended Danish-American folk schools. Even so, the schools greatly influenced Danish-American communities. They helped perpetuate Danish culture and at the same time recognized the need for Danes to adapt to American society.

Ethnic Organizations

Danish Americans began forming ethnic organizations in the 1860s to provide companionship and aid to immigrants newly arrived from the old country. Today, some of these organizations still exist, though their goal

Danish Americans gather in Minneapolis for a 1926 ethnic festival. The banners represent various fraternal organizations.

has shifted as interest has grown in keeping alive the Danish heritage. Many, though, continue to provide personal services such as life insurance, medical assistance, health care, and burial aid. These organizations also sponsor social gatherings, dances, picnics, and sporting activities.

At first, Danish Americans were so few in number that instead of banding together in their own groups they joined those open to all Scandinavians. The oldest such organization is Dania. Founded in Chicago in 1862 and open to all Scandinavian Americans, its original function was to provide health insurance for its members in an era when it was not yet available through employers or the government. Soon Dania changed its character. As the number of Danish immigrants grew, the organization became exclusively Danish, and eventually many of its functions were taken over by separate clubs. Dania and the Dania Ladies Society of Chicago are still active and have inspired the founding of similar organizations in Racine, Wisconsin (1867), Oakland, California (1867), and Brooklyn, New York (1886). Dania of California and its women's auxiliary, Dannebrog, are statewide organizations with chapters in almost every large city. Membership peaked in 1930, with 3,289 members. In 1979, the number had fallen

This 1927 Minneapolis festival featured a horse-drawn platform bearing young Danish Americans costumed in Old World clothing.

The drill team of the Chicago Danish Brotherhood poses in 1926, seven years after the organization changed its rules and allowed English to be spoken at meetings.

to about 1,000 but the club continues to support a home for the aged in San Rafael, California.

The largest Danish ethnic organization is the Danish Brotherhood of America, founded in 1882. Like Dania, it started as a group insurance program, though it was limited to Danish-American veterans. Before long, the Brotherhood dedicated itself to the preservation of Danish culture. At first its meetings were open only to men, were held in secret, and sometimes included initiation ceremonies that drew criticism from the Danish-American clergy. Still, the Brotherhood grew rapidly. A branch was even founded in Copenhagen; Lodge No. 318 served immigrants returning from the United States.

Over the years the Danish Brotherhood evolved greatly, relaxing its standards to conform to changes occurring within the Danish-American community at large. By 1910, even persons who could not speak Danish—though they had to understand it—were admitted into the organization. In 1919, the rules were changed again—discussion in English was allowed under certain circumstances. By 1931, language requirements were dropped altogether and prospective members needed only to have one parent of Danish descent to be eligible for admission. Finally, in 1939, men married to Danish women were allowed to become social members of the Brotherhood.

In 1977, the Danish Brotherhood had more than 150 lodges in 26 states, Canada, and Denmark. Headquartered in Omaha, Nebraska, the Brotherhood maintains a membership exceeding more than 11,000. In addition to sponsoring social functions and classes, it publishes a national monthly magazine, *American Dane*, and a newsletter, *Viking Adventures*.

A third ethnic organization, the American-Scandinavian Foundation, has promoted goodwill between America and Scandinavian countries since 1910. One of its principal benefactors was Niels Poulson (1843–1911), an immigrant from Copenhagen who arrived in America in 1864 and became the owner of the Hecla Architectural Iron Works, a Brooklyn, New York, plant specializing in ornamental iron- and steelwork. Hecla's many projects included the ornamental work for New York City's two huge central railroad depots, Grand Central Terminal and Pennsylvania Station.

Poulson bequeathed his fortune—more than $500,000—to the American-Scandinavian Foundation. To this day, the foundation provides scholarships for research, sponsors translation contests, hosts cultural exhibits, and offers charter flights to Scandinavian countries. In 1913 the organization began publishing a quarterly magazine—*American-Scandinavian Review*—that continues to feature the work of many Danish and Danish-American authors.

Sophus Neble edited Den Danske Pioneer *in Omaha, Nebraska. The paper was banned in Denmark after Neble wrote, "America has given us the bread and freedom that our fatherland denied us."*

Publications

The Danes' small population, their lack of community feeling, and their desire to shed attachments with their native land all stood in the way of a healthy and lasting Danish-American press. Indeed the ethnic group never had a daily newspaper, and many of the 50 or so weeklies survived only a few years. Danish-American newspapers were not widely supported, on the whole, and as time wore on interest in them steadily dwindled. In 1910, the combined circulation of the 7 leading papers totaled 72,000, but by 1920 this number had declined to 37,800.

Nevertheless, the few Danish-American papers that existed served a valuable function. They helped immigrants become acclimated to their adopted country and, at the same time, kept them in touch with events in the homeland. Furthermore, the press sought to lend cohesiveness to the community by reporting its opinions and activities. Greenhorn immigrants, who seldom spoke English, especially relied on the papers, which were their only source of printed news.

The largest and longest-lasting Danish-American paper, *Den Danske Pioneer* (The Danish Pioneer), was founded in Omaha in 1872 by Mark Hansen, a colorful figure who rode to work on a horse. The publication reached its peak circulation—more than 39,000—in 1914 and is still being issued today. Though Hansen himself never wrote a word of copy, he gave the paper its tone by determining what news it printed. Thus,

At its peak, the publishing house owned by Christian Rasmussen issued four newspapers and three magazines.

although *Den Danske Pioneer* regularly reported on social, political, and cultural activities within the Danish-American community, church events went virtually unrecorded.

The paper's next editor, Sophus Neble, continued this anticlerical approach but added an important new slant. He often touted America and contrasted the virtues of its political course with the conservative policies of Denmark's king. At one point Neble wrote, "America has given us the bread and freedom that our fatherland denied us." Neble's criticisms angered the Danish government, and from 1886 to 1898 the paper was banned from the Danish mail. In 1925, however, Neble was knighted by the Danish monarch, not for his political opinions, but for his tireless work aiding needy members of the Danish-American community.

One other Danish-American paper is still being published: *Bien* (The Bee), a bilingual weekly based in

The Danish Lutheran Publishing House, headquartered in Blair, Nebraska, no longer stands.

Los Angeles. Founded in San Francisco in 1882, *Bien* reached its peak circulation in 1940, when it claimed 5,000 subscribers. Initially, the paper catered to a readership composed mainly of immigrants, providing them with essential news and information about the new land. As the readership became increasingly used to living in America, it grew more interested in features about life in the old country. Finally, the paper's format changed once again, featuring lengthy stories about ethnic group activities around the country. In the early 1980s *Bien*'s circulation was approximately 3,500.

The best-known Danish American involved in journalism was Christian Rasmussen (1852–1926), the "Danish Newspaper King." He owned four papers, three magazines, and an advertising agency. A conservative Republican, he held views that won assent in the Midwest, where his publications sold most briskly. Rasmussen's printing plants also issued many Danish and Norwegian books. None of his enterprises lasted into the 1980s.

Because ethnic publications tend to be short-lived, in 1976 the Danish American Language Foundation

These dancers, photographed in 1937, anticipated the folk revival of ethnic customs later shared by the entire Danish-American community.

was established to help maintain the three surviving organs: the newspapers *Den Danske Pioneer* and *Bien*, and a semimonthly religious publication, *Kirke og Folk* (Church and People). Funds for the foundation were collected in Denmark in recognition of the American Bicentennial.

Though few Danish-American publications became permanent fixtures in the community, they served an important function. By preserving the language and providing news from Denmark, they helped immigrants remain identified with their ethnic group. At the same time, these papers encouraged Danish Americans to learn about the political and social aspects of their new country. Their influence cannot be measured by numbers, but by the important bridge they formed between the Old World and the New.

Foreign Exchange

In addition to keeping alive old customs, Danish Americans enthusiastically foster close ties between their ancestral homeland and their adopted one. One place where Danes and Americans gather is Skovsoen Danish Language Village, located on Lake Morgan, near Menahga, Minnesota. Each summer, a summer camp there hosts boys and girls, ages 8 to 17, who come from the United States, Canada, and Denmark. A Danish village is created on campgrounds, and North American youngsters are given Danish names. Even Lake Morgan is renamed "Nyhavn," after a rowdy sailors' district in Copenhagen. American and Danish counselors hold classes in the Danish language, culture, history, and customs. "Villagers" eat only Danish foods and take part in activities that include nature hikes, *folkedans* (folk dancing), and a Danish Christmas celebration.

The grandest celebration uniting America and Denmark occurs on American Independence Day, July 4, which is observed not only in the United States, but also in Denmark, the only other nation in the world that celebrates American independence. The idea was

In 1909, Dr. Max Henius, a biochemist, organized a Danish-American reunion festival in Aarhus, Denmark. It has since become an annual event.

the brainchild of Dr. Max Henius (1859–1935), a biochemist who was born in Aalborg, Denmark, and immigrated to Chicago. In 1909, he organized a Danish-American reunion festival in Aarhus, Denmark. On July 4 of that year, more than 1,000 Danish Americans celebrated with an even greater number of Danes. The event was so successful that Henius proposed making it an annual event. Danish Americans responded by collecting money and purchasing 200 acres of heather-covered hills outside the Danish city of Aalborn. The area was named the Rebild National Park, and since 1912 Danes and Danish Americans have gathered there every July 4. The Danes' Worldwide Archives are located nearby, along with an immigrant museum that houses many letters sent from America by early settlers from Denmark.

Many Danish Americans annually visit the Old Country and return with the handicrafts for which Denmark is justly celebrated. Danish silver and linens are beautifully designed, as is the furniture made from orange teak, deep-brown rosewood, and blond pine. Handmade glassware from Denmark's Holmegaard factory and porcelain by Royal Copenhagen or Bing and Grondahl are also admired throughout the world. Most of these items are streamlined and functional, and they give American homes an atmosphere that is *hyggelig*—"comfortable and cozy."

Festivals and Holidays

Like other ethnic groups, Danish Americans have recently felt compelled to preserve the tradition and customs of their ancestral land. Toward this end, they celebrate certain milestones in Danish history. On June 5, for example, the Danish Constitution Day is observed annually in several American communities including Chicago; Minneapolis; Croton, New York; and San Rafael, California. Other towns with significant Danish-American populations hold annual festivals that feature gymnastics, folk dancing, and Danish foods.

No festival compares with the "Danish Days" held during the third week in September in Solvang, California. Founded in 1910, the town of Solvang was the site of one of the original folk high schools. Since World War II it has been transformed into a vision of Old Denmark and a popular tourist attraction. Visitors inspect the town's windmills and half-timbered cottages, which have storks perched on their thatched roofs, then stroll along streets lined with shops and bakeries and relax in Tivoli Square, named for Copenhagen's world-famous amusement park.

Christmas is celebrated in the Danish-American home by reenacting Old World traditions. The season begins on December 1, when children open their first gift, commemorating Advent, the beginning of the Christian year. Small gifts are then exchanged each day until Christmas Eve. On that occasion, the family gathers for a traditional dinner consisting of roast goose or duck, glazed potatoes, and red cabbage. The dessert, rice pudding, conceals an almond; whoever finds it wins a prize. Afterward, the gifts are opened around a family tree decorated with hearts, cones, apples, angels, and other handmade ornaments. Figures representing *Nisser*, bearded Christmas elves, appear on the tree, on tablecloths, and on hanging linens. At night, the celebrants circle the tree, joining hands and singing traditional Danish Christmas songs.

At other celebrations, Danish Americans drink *akvavit*, a clear liquor flavored with caraway seeds. It is frequently served with *smorrebrod*, the traditional open-faced sandwiches. When making a toast, Danish Americans lift a glass of akvavit, look into each other's eyes, then salute each other by saying, *Skaal*! (Cheers!). ✎

Danish modern furniture—universally admired for its streamlined design—adorns many American homes.

*In the 1890s, crusading
journalist Jacob Riis shocked
Americans with his blistering
reports of inner-city slum life.*

MAKING THEIR MARK

Just as the first Danish immigrants smoothly adapted to American ways, so have their descendants found many areas of achievement open to them. They seldom face the opposition that deterred the progress of other ethnic groups. Because their easy entry into the mainstream has given the group a low profile, however, the considerable accomplishments of Danish Americans often go unnoticed by their neighbors.

Some Grand Successes

One of the most influential of all Danish Americans was Jacob August Riis, a journalist and social reformer. Born in 1849 in Ribe, an ancient city on Denmark's west coast, Riis attended the private school where his father taught. He left school at the age of 15 and went to Copenhagen, where he was apprenticed to a carpenter. In 1870, his taste for adventure led him to the United States. He arrived with only $40 in his pocket and for the next three years struggled to make ends meet, taking on odd jobs. In 1873, a New York City news association hired him as a reporter and Riis quickly demonstrated his talent for finding meaty stories. He then started his own newspaper, a one-man operation published in Brooklyn. In 1877, he became a reporter for a major New York paper, the *Daily Trib-*

Victor Borge, a refugee of Nazi-occupied Denmark, amused American audiences with his comic routines at the piano.

une, covering crime and slum life. His stories, with their wealth of closely observed detail and moral passion, gained a wide following. In the 1880s, his accounts of New York's squalid, unhealthy tenements featured gripping photographs that today are on display in the Museum of the City of New York. Another major New York paper, *The Evening Sun*, wooed Riis to its staff in 1890, the same year he published his searing account of urban slums, *How the Other Half Lives*. A dozen books followed, as did a profusion of magazine articles. Riis's fame continued to spread as he lectured nationwide about the evils of tenement housing and the need for legislative reform and community action.

In his stirring autobiography, *The Making of an American*, published in 1901, Riis stated that he first became outraged by squalid housing as a boy. Even in Ribe, an idyllic town, poor people lived bleakly. Riis's discovery was not unusual, but his decision to do something about it was. At the age of 13 he personally cleaned up local tenements and exterminated rodents. This willingness to act never left Riis, and by the time of his death in 1914 he had helped improve the lot of slum dwellers, causing the destruction of New York City's Mulberry Bend, an especially wretched area. Though he had many political enemies, one of Riis's strongest supporters was his good friend President Theodore Roosevelt, the 26th president of the United States, who once called Riis "the best American I have ever known."

Jacob Riis alerted Americans to the hidden squalor of modern life. Another, equally renowned Danish American accomplished a more cheerful feat, awakening Americans to unexpected sources of gaiety and humor. Victor Borge—his real name is Borge Rosenbaum—was born in Denmark in 1909. As a child, he showed promise on the piano and studied for the concert stage, but soon it was apparent that he also had a gift for making people laugh. He combined his two talents and became a musical comic. During World War

II, Borge frequently aimed his jokes at the Nazi party, which had come into power in Germany under Adolf Hitler. Annoyed by Borge's irreverence, the Nazis repeatedly threatened his life. Undaunted, Borge hired a bodyguard and kept up his comic assault. In 1940, in the early days of World War II, Germany invaded Denmark. Fortunately, Borge was in Stockholm, Sweden, and escaped from there to the United States with his American wife.

In the United States, Borge learned English by watching films in New York's entertainment district, 42nd Street. "For 15 cents I could see three movies," he later recalled. "Sometimes I sat there for 20 hours, hearing them over and over." Noting that those same movie houses have since turned into X-rated theaters, Borge said, "Of course they're not the kind of movies they show now on 42nd Street. Otherwise I probably would have stayed even longer."

Borge's gentle humor and unpredictable shenanigans at the piano gained him a new audience in America. His act was frequently improvised, but often included regular routines such as eating a sandwich during a 64-bar rest in a concerto or playing a frenzied duet with a partner that involved running around the piano and wrestling for the keyboard. Such antics made Borge one of America's best-loved entertainers. He often gave performances at Carnegie Hall, and through the 1950s and 1960s he appeared on television, at one time hosting his own program. Part clown, part satirist, Borge eludes strict classification. One critic has called him a "philosopher, linguist, historian and woolgatherer."

Another Danish-American entertainer, Jean Hersholt, was born in 1886 in Copenhagen to parents who both acted with the Danish Folk Theater. Hersholt immigrated to America in 1912, entertaining on ship to pay his way. Upon his arrival, he began a career in a medium then in its infancy—motion pictures. At the time movies were silent, so many foreign actors found work with the major studios. A problem arose, however, in 1927, when *The Jazz Story*, the first commercial sound movie, was released, breaking box office records. Thereafter, major studios switched to sound production and many actors—native-born and foreign—were put out of work, often because the crude microphones used on the set distorted their voices. Hersholt was one of the few to manage the transition to "talkies," and he appeared in such popular films as *The Country Doctor* (1936) and the three-part series about *Dr. Christian* (1940–1941). All told, Hersholt was featured in more than 400 movies.

Yet Hersholt is even better known for his accomplishments as a humanitarian. During World War II, he was active in America Relief, Inc., an organization that helped Danish refugees in Sweden. In 1939, the film industry awarded him a special Oscar for his many altruistic achievements. These included founding Alderso, the first Danish home for the aged, and also the California Denmark Home Foundation, which enabled elderly immigrants to visit their native country. In 1949, he was given another special Oscar for his work as president of the Motion Picture Relief Fund. Hersholt was also president of the Academy of Motion Picture Arts and Sciences for four years. In his honor, the Motion Picture Academy annually bestows the Jean Hersholt Humanitarian Award to the industry member who best continues Hersholt's philanthropic efforts.

In America no art form has lately gained a larger following than dance. And one of its most celebrated performers, choreographers, and administrators is Peter Martins. He was born in Copenhagen in 1946 and studied there with the world-renowned Royal Danish Ballet, joining the company as a dancer in 1965. Two years later, he was appointed soloist. In 1969, the dance troupe went on an American tour and Martins came to the attention of the New York City Ballet, headed by the innovative choreographer George Balanchine, a Russian American. Eager to work with Balanchine, Martins immigrated to the United States and became a principal dancer with the New York company. His work with Balanchine brought Martins international fame. Known for his coolly elegant style, Martins enlivened many of Balanchine's works, including *Piano Works* by Schuman, *David's Bundlertanze*, and *Union*

Jean Hersholt (center) acted in more than 400 films, including The Country Doctor, *and won a special Oscar in 1939 for his many humanitarian deeds.*

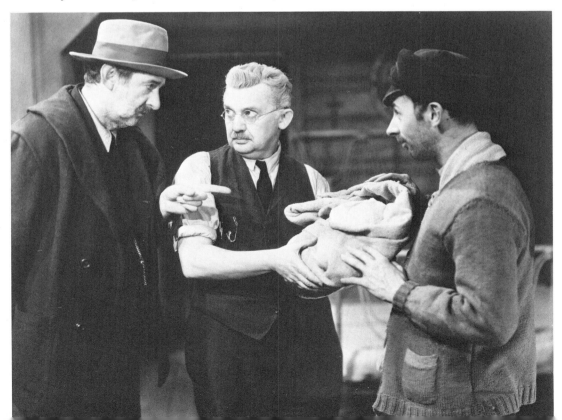

Jack, in which Martins caused a sensation by dancing with a cigarette dangling from his mouth.

A gifted choreographer, Martins created his first ballet, *Calcium Light Night*, in 1977. For the next five years, he continued both to perform and choreograph, then concentrated completely on the latter, winning great acclaim for the more than 30 ballets he has produced. After Balanchine's death in 1983, the New York City Ballet named Martins its codirector (sharing the post with choreographer Jerome Robbins). Martins's experiences in America are recounted in his autobiography, *Far From Denmark*.

Long before Martins began to explore the mobility of the human body, another Danish American, sculptor Gutzon Borglum, made a memorable study of the human face. Borglum was born in 1867 in Idaho on the ranch owned by his father, a physician who had emigrated from Denmark. As a boy, Gutzon developed a keen interest in art. He studied first at a San Francisco academy, then went to Paris, attending Julian's academy and the Ecole des Beaux-Arts. He returned to the United States in 1901, settling in New York City. Soon he was commissioned by the federal government to sculpt a likeness of Lincoln for the U.S. Capitol in Washington, D.C. He then received more commissions, creating a statue of the clergyman and antislavery leader Henry Ward Beecher; the mythological sculpture *Mares of Diomedes*, which now is on display at the Metropolitan Museum in New York City; and figures that adorn New York City's largest Episcopal cathedral, St. John the Divine.

In 1916, Borglum was at work on a Confederate memorial on Stone Mountain, Georgia, when World War I broke out, interrupting the project. In 1924, he resumed it, only to be interrupted again, this time because of his disagreements with the association that hired him to execute the work. Borglum then moved on to his greatest assignment, supervising one of the most enormous art sculptures of all time: the Mount Rushmore National Memorial in South Dakota. From

1927 until his death, Borglum oversaw the design, engineering, and sculpting of four presidential heads—those of Presidents George Washington, Thomas Jefferson, Abraham Lincoln, and Theodore Roosevelt—carved out of the sheer rock of the Black Hills. Under Borglum's guidance, workmen used small models to calculate the measurements of the finished monument, then shaped the stone with drills and dynamite. The result was a statue whose figures are larger than any others in the world. Each head is at least 60 feet tall (George Washington's is as high as a five-story building) and chipped out of sheer rock.

The project was nearly completed when Borglum died in 1941. His son, Lincoln Borglum, then supervised its final stages. Today, Mount Rushmore ranks among the wonders of the American landscape, and millions of visitors make the pilgrimage to South Dakota to marvel at Borglum's titanic feat. A man of extraordinary vision and vitality, Borglum once expressed

Peter Martins starred with the New York City Ballet before becoming its codirector in 1983.

the wish that the immense faces he created would last "until the wind and the rain alone shall wear them away."

An artist who worked on a smaller scale was Emil Carlsen. He was born in 1853 in Copenhagen, where he studied architecture at the Royal Academy of Fine Arts. At the age of 19, he immigrated to America, finding work in Chicago as a painter's assistant. He then decided to create original works, inspired by a trip to Paris that brought him into contact with the still lifes of the 18th-century artist Jean Baptiste Simeon Chardin. Carlsen set about learning his craft, mastering the subtleties of light and color in scenes of nature that ranged from still lifes of flowers to dramatic landscapes and seascapes featuring billowing clouds and distant shorelines. One of his favorite locations was Skagen, on the northern tip of the Jutland peninsula.

At first Carlsen was unknown and struggled in poverty. But eventually his efforts won the recognition of critics, viewers, and painters, who soon ranked him among the leading American Impressionists. A particularly memorable work, *The South Strand*, hangs in the National Museum of Art in Washington, D.C. Carlsen's canvases also grace the collections of the National Gallery in Washington, D.C., and the Metropolitan

Gutzon Borglum, pictured here on Mount Rushmore, hoped that the four presidential faces he designed for the monument would endure "until the wind and rain alone shall wear them away."

Emil Carlsen's paintings rank among the masterpieces of American Impressionism.

Museum of Art in New York City. As recently as 1975, 43 years after his death, Carlsen's work was featured at an exhibit at the Rowe Gallery in San Francisco. A gifted teacher, Carlsen taught for a number of years at the Pennsylvania Academy of Fine Arts.

A much different story was that of William S. Knudsen, who rose from the post of stock clerk in a bicycle plant to the presidency of General Motors, one of America's largest corporations. Born in 1879 in Copenhagen, Wilhelm Signius Knudsen attended a technical school operated by the government, training to become a coppersmith. In 1900, he immigrated to America, settling in New York City, where he worked in a shipyard and a locomotive shop. He then became a clerk for the John R. Keim bicycle manufacturing plant, an ideal employer because it soon shifted into the production of automobile parts, a rapidly growing industry. At Keim, Knudsen showed signs of managerial brilliance by quickly rising to the position of factory production manager. In 1911, the plant was purchased by the Ford Motor Company and Knudsen was transferred to Ford headquarters. Within 10 years, he had

General Motors president William S. Knudsen donated his services to the American government in World War II. His efforts earned him the highest rank ever awarded an American civilian—lieutenant general.

been appointed chief of production of all Ford plants. In 1922, Knudsen left Ford and became an adviser for General Motors Corporation. Two years later he became president and general manager of GM's Chevrolet subsidiary. Under his leadership, the Chevrolet became one of America's most popular automobiles. In 1937, Knudsen was chosen president of General Motors.

Knudsen's outstanding abilities were recognized by President Franklin Roosevelt, who appointed him general director of the Office of Production Management. This agency was responsible for coordinating and mobilizing America's manpower and industrial resources during World War II. Under Knudsen's direction, American steel plants set a new production record, plans were completed for doubling aluminum production, and the government accumulated large stockpiles of rubber and tin. Knudsen performed this vital service for the grand salary of $1 a year, in effect donating his expertise as an act of patriotism. For his contributions, Knudsen was made a lieutenant general in the army, the first civilian in the nation's history to be so honored. No 20th-century Danish American exemplifies the immigrant dream more spectacularly than William S. Knudsen.

Quiet Gains

It seems in keeping with the story of Danish Americans that one of their number could create a major symbol of the United States—Mount Rushmore—yet few people would ever know his name. As a group, Danish immigrants were equally vital in shaping their adopted homeland, but their contributions often remained in the background. Few in number, spread thinly throughout the country, and eager to fit into the American mainstream, they never formed a cohesive community that could build stable ethnic institutions, and their schools, newspapers, and neighborhoods soon blended into a larger American identity.

At the same time, the Danish-American experience is a triumph of adjustment and adaptation. True, they had many advantages. They were white, Protestant, and relatively well educated. They came from a country with a democratic tradition that primed them to participate in America's political system. And because they immigrated for economic reasons, Danes knew that the more quickly they shed their uniqueness, the more quickly they would prosper.

Even so, their transition was not accomplished without effort. Danish immigrants had lived in a small, homogeneous country with a long history and well-established traditions. To them, America seemed huge, undeveloped, and a bit frightening. They sacrificed much of their ancient heritage in order to make their way in the New World, and in recent times have been forced to work harder than other groups to recover their ethnicity.

Unlike some other immigrant communities, Danish Americans introduced little of their own culture to the New World. Instead, they played an important role in defining the emerging American nation, a nation forged out of the dreams of its immigrants. ≈

FURTHER READING

Friis, Erik J., ed. *The Scandinavian Presence in America*. New York: Harper's Magazine Press, 1973.

Georg, Anders, and Ole Kjaer Madsen, eds. *Denmark—USA: 200 Years of Close Relations*. Copenhagen: Royal Danish Ministry of Foreign Affairs, 1976.

Hale, Frederic. *Danes in America*. Seattle: University of Washington Press, 1984.

Hvidt, Kristian. *Flight to America*. New York: Academic Press, 1975.

MacHaffle, Ingeborg S., and Margaret A. Nielsen. *Of Danish Ways*. Minneapolis: Dillon Press, 1976.

Nielsen, George R. *The Danish Americans*. Boston: Twayne Publishers, 1981.

Paulsen, Frank M. *Danish Settlements on the Canadian Prairies*. Ottawa: National Museums of Canada, 1974.

Zafris, Nancy. "American Shores." *American Dane*, September 1982, 19–20.

INDEX

PICTURE CREDITS

We would like to thank the following sources for providing photographs: AP/ Wide World Photos: p. 31; Archives of American Art, Smithsonian Institution, Washington, D.C.: p. 103; The Bettmann Archive: pp. 16–17, 21, 24, 34–35, 104; Copenhagen Bymuseum: pp. 26, 28; Dana College, Blair, Nebraska: p. 78; Danes Worldwide Archives: cover, pp. 69, 73, 76, 87, 88; Danish Immigration Museum: pp. 58, 83, 86, 89; Danish Tourist Board: pp. 49, 51(bottom); Dansk Folkmuseum: p. 27; Gurtman and Murtha Associates: p. 98; Mrs. Elia Hansen, Institute of Texan Cultures: pp. 64–65, 66; *Harper's Weekly*, November 7, 1894: p. 43; Erich Hartmann/Magnum: pp. 50, 51(top); The Huntington Library, San Marino, California: p. 39; Institute of Texan Cultures: pp. 45, 46; King Merrill: pp. 54(top & bottom), 55; Arhus Kunst Museum, Denmark: pp. 52–53; Library of Congress: pp. 25, 29, 36, 44, 47, 48, 57, 91; Joan Liffring-Zug: p. 57; Lolland-Falsters Stiftsmuseum: p. 41; H. D. Madsen, Institute of Texan Cultures: p. 61; Minnesota Historical Society: pp. 12–13, 70, 82, 84, 85, 90; Musee des Arts Decoratifs de Montreal: p. 93; Museum of Modern Art, Film Stills Archives: p. 99; National Archives: p. 81; National History Museum, Fredericksburg, Virginia: p. 23; National Museum of Copenhagen: p. 18; Nebraska State Historical Society: pp. 68, 71, 77; New York Public Library, Rare Book Division: p. 37; Verner A. Petersen, Institute of Texan Cultures: pp. 59, 62; The Royal Library, Copenhagen: p. 38; *San Antonio Light* Collection, Institute of Texan Cultures: p. 14; State Historical Society of Wisconsin: p. 74; Taurus Photos: p. 20; The Toledo Museum of Art: p. 22; UPI/Bettmann Newsphotos: pp. 30, 32, 33; Utah State Historical Society: pp. 40, 42, 67, 72.

MARK MUSSARI, a writer and teacher, has contributed to the *Macmillan Reader* and taught at Villanova University. A member of the Danish Brotherhood in America, he lives near Philadelphia.

DANIEL PATRICK MOYNIHAN is the senior United States senator from New York. He is also the only person in American history to serve in the cabinets or subcabinets of four successive presidents—Kennedy, Johnson, Nixon, and Ford. Formerly a professor of government at Harvard University, he has written and edited many books, including *Beyond the Melting Pot, Ethnicity: Theory and Experience* (both with Nathan Glazer), *Loyalties,* and *Family and Nation.*